BRITANNICA BOOKS

Animals All Around

pi kids®

An imprint of Phoenix International Publications, Inc

Chicago • London • New York • Hamburg • Mexico City • Sydney

Rainforest

Tropical rainforests are found in regions of the tropics where temperatures are always high and where about 70 to 100 inches or more of rain falls evenly throughout the year.

An **anteater** catches insects with its long, sticky, wormlike tongue. It lives in Central and South America. Find one in the rainforest scene.

Butterflies live on every continent except Antarctica. How many butterflies can you find?

Parrots are found mainly in the warm southern half of the world. You can identify a parrot by its bright feathers and noisy call. Spot the parrot here.

Sloths are known for moving very sl-o-o-owly in the trees of Central and South America. Can you spot one in the trees?

The **toucan** lives high in the trees of Central and South America and has a large, brightly colored bill. Look for the toucan.

Did you know?

Tropical rainforests are just one kind of rainforest. Thick forests in other wet areas of the world are also called rainforests.

Savanna

A **savanna** is a large flat area of land with grass and very few trees. This scene shows an African savanna, but they can be found on other continents as well. Most savannas grow in tropical regions. Conditions are warm to hot in all seasons. Rain falls only during a few months each year.

The **wildebeest**, or gnu, is a species of antelope that lives on the African savanna. Can you find these wildebeests in the herd?

Did you know?

Human beings first appeared on the African savanna before spreading to other continents.

Coral Reef

A **coral reef** is a ridge of coral, algae, sand, and mud, formed in shallow ocean areas. Often called the "rainforests of the sea," coral reefs are home to a spectacular variety of plants and animals.

An **anemone** looks like an underwater flower. Do you see an anemone that looks like this?

The largest **angelfish** grow to be 18 inches long. Is there an angelfish in this underwater scene?

The **clown fish** makes its home among the tentacles of a sea anemone. Can you spot a clown fish here?

A **crab** moves usually by walking or crawling, though some crabs are good swimmers. Do you see a crab on the reef?

The **puffer fish** can inflate itself with water or air until it is as round as a globe. Do you see a puffed-up puffer fish in this scene?

The **sea star**'s older common name is "starfish," but it is an invertebrate, not a fish. Look for the sea star here.

Did you know?

A coral reef may grow into a permanent coral island.

Swamp

A **swamp** is a wetland ecosystem with waterlogged ground and plant life dominated by trees. Swamps are often found in low-lying regions with rivers that supply the water.

Alligators are large animals with powerful tails that are used both in defense and in swimming. Spot the alligator here.

A **frog** has smooth, moist skin and big, bulging eyes. It catches prey by flicking out its long, sticky tongue. Find a frog in the swamp scene.

A **heron** is a long-legged wading bird. It stands very still like a statue in the water while looking for food. Do you see a heron wading here?

A **river otter** has short legs, a strong neck, and a long flattened tail. Can you find an otter in this scene?

A **turtle**'s bony shell is an adaptation that protects it from predators. Find a turtle here.

Did you know?

Swamps are found throughout the world.

At Night

Bats roost during the day and forage at night. Animals that are active at night are called *nocturnal* animals.

The **badger** uses its heavy claws to dig for food. Spot the badger here.

Male **crickets** produce musical chirping sounds. Can you find a cricket in this scene?

The Virginia, or common, **opossum** eats almost anything, including insects, eggs, small mammals, and fruit. Look for the opossum here.

An **owl** is most active at dusk and at dawn. Do you see an owl in this scene?

Intelligent and inquisitive, the **raccoon** swims and climbs readily. Can you find a raccoon here?

Did you know?

Bats are important to humans because they eat insects, pollinate plants, and scatter seeds.

Forest

A **forest** is a complex ecosystem in which trees are the dominant life-form. Animals that live in forests have highly developed hearing, and many are adapted for vertical (up and down) movement through the environment.

Because of their large size, **bears** have few natural enemies in the wild. Look for the bear.

In all but one deer species (reindeer), only the male **deer** have antlers. Can you spot a male deer here?

A **fox** is a member of the dog family. Is there a fox in this picture?

Moose are bold and readily defend themselves against large carnivores. Look for a moose here.

Skunks are also called polecats. Can you find a skunk in the forest scene?

Wolf pups are born in the spring, usually in a den consisting of a natural hole or burrow. Look for the wolf pup here.

Did you know?

Forests are among the most complex ecosystems in the world. An ecosystem is all the living and nonliving things in a certain area.

Desert

A **desert** is any large, extremely dry area of land with sparse vegetation. Deserts are home to distinctive plants and animals specially adapted to the harsh environment.

An **armadillo** uses its keen sense of smell to locate food. Spot the armadillo here.

Hares like the **jackrabbit** live in North America, Europe, Asia, and Africa. Do you see a jackrabbit?

Many **scorpions** live in deserts around the world. These animals are relatives of spiders. Find three in the desert scene.

Flying makes **roadrunners** tired, so they prefer to dash around on their powerful legs. How many roadrunners can you find?

The **sidewinder** snake gets its name from the way it moves in the sand. Can you spot a sidewinder in the sand?

Most **tortoises** are vegetarians and eat foliage, flowers, and fruits. Look for a tortoise here.

Did you know?

Desert animals are active during the brief, infrequent wet periods and inactive during the usually dry times.

Arctic Lands

Arctic lands lie in cold, northern regions, where the ground is permanently frozen in many areas.

Caribou (or reindeer) have deeply cloven hoofs that let their feet spread on snow or soft ground. Is there a caribou here?

The **musk ox** is a stocky mammal with a large head, short neck, and short, stout legs. Can you find one in this snowy scene?

Polar bear cubs are born during the winter in a den of ice or snow. Look for the bear cub.

 Puffins nest in large colonies on seaside and island cliffs. Can you spot a puffin here?

In the wild, a **walrus** can live more than 40 years. Find a walrus in this picture.

 The **wolverine** looks like a small, squat bear and is known for its strength, cunning, and fearlessness. Look for a wolverine.

Did you know?

White fur or feathers allow some northern animals to blend into snowy landscapes in order to hide from prey or to protect themselves from predators.

Ramble back to the **rainforest** and find these eight monkeys:

Stampede back to the **savanna** to find these amazing animals:

ostrich

lion

rhinoceros

cheetah

zebra

Swim back to the **coral reef** and find these sea turtles:

Slip back to the **swamp** to find these insects:

dragonfly

butterfly

spider

beetle

ladybug

Fly back to the **nighttime** scene and find 10 fireflies.

Flip back and find these **forest** dwellers:

butterfly

woodpecker

opossum

mouse

chipmunk

bee

Dash back to the **desert** to find these lizards:

Sled back to the **Arctic lands** to find these well-hidden inhabitants:

ermine

wolf

hare

snowy owl

polar fox

harp seal pup